MAKE MORE WORK LESS by Creating your Gateway to STARDOM

Skillset Diversification, **T**ame Stress, **A**ssess Risk, **R**aise Wealth, and **DOM**inate the Unknown!

**Make More Work Less by Creating your Gateway to STARDOM
Skillset Diversification, Tame Stress, Assess Risk, Raise Wealth, and DOMinate the Unknown**

Published by
10-10-10 Publishing
1-9225 Leslie Street
Richmond Hill
Ontario, Canada
L3B 3H6

Copyright © March 2018
by Fong Chua and Jessica Ng
Edmonton, Alberta, Canada
www.makemoreworklessbook.com/STARDOM

All Rights Reserved. No part of this book may be reproduced in any form, by photocopying or by electronic or mechanical means, including information storage or retrieval systems, without permission in writing from both the copyright owner and the publisher of this book. The opinions and conclusions drawn in this book are solely those of the author. The author and the publisher bear no liability in connection with the use of the ideas presented.

For information about special discounts for bulk purchases, please contact 10-10-10 Publishing at 1-888-504-6257.

Printed in the United States of America

ISBN-13: 978-1986906470 (paperback)
ISBN-10: 1986906477

First Edition

- For Additional Content -

Visit us at:

www.yourarea.ca
www.meetfongchua.com
www.makemoreworklessbook.com

Social Media:

Facebook: @FongChua
            @AssuranceRealEstateAcquisitionsInc
Youtube Channel: yourAREATV
Twitter: Fong Chua
LinkedIn: Fong Chua
Featured on Results Radio
Video Series: MakeMoreMindBites

Books:

Make More Work Less:
The Guide to Unlocking Your Potential to Live and Work on Your Own Terms

Make More Work Less with Cashflow:
The Step-by-Step Keys to Finding, Acquiring, and Maintaining Cashflow Investment Properties

Make More Work Less by Building a Team:
The Secrets to Selecting, Building, and Maintaining an Ultimate Power Team

All Make More Work Less books are available on amazon or connect with Fong Chua at www.meetfongchua.com.

- ABOUT THE AUTHORS -

Assurance Real Estate Acquisitions Inc. was brought together by the managing partners, Jessica Ng and Fong Chua, to bring to life their beliefs in adding value to people. This partnership specializes in uniting the right people, the right project, and the right solution, all while adding value to all those involved, creating a win-win environment. Assurance Real Estate Acquisitions Inc. places great emphasis on relational capital, which is why they treat their clients and partners the same as their loved ones.

Starting out as engineers and winners of the Deal Makers, Loyalty, Results, and Human Relations Awards, Fong and Jessica have the technical skills, attention to detail, and the passion to add value, to ensure that all projects are of value for all parties involved and that all relationships are valued. Whether it is coaching clients to great results, joint venturing on projects, sharing their business and real estate expertise with others, or giving back to the community, Fong and Jessica adds value beyond what is expected and the results speak for itself. When it comes to partnerships, three words describe their focus: loyalty, relationships, and results. This is why they believe that partners and clients should be for life.

Our Mission: To bring wealth, be it financial, knowledge or security, to all those who seek it. With our expertise and heart, it is our mission to impact as many people as we can by showing them how they can achieve more than they think.

This book is dedicated to:

Our family and friends who motivates us, encourages us, and reminds us that there are many people who could use our guidance, and that by sharing our knowledge, will lead them to greater success.

Our coach, JT Foxx, who inspires, motivates, and believes in us. He reminds us each day that we can strive to be more and to always add value to others.

Each other, without the support and dedication that we committed to our business and to each other, our ventures would not be possible.

- ACKNOWLEDGEMENTS -

We would like to acknowledge and thank all those involved with the publishing of this book for their hard work and care in putting this book together. We are absolutely thankful for their patience and time spent dealing with our requests.

Thank you to everyone that supported us in this venture: from cover design (Jong Chua, Just Creative Inc.), to photography (Krzysztof Wisniewski, Krisskiphotography), to content organization (Ryan Falkenberg), and to guidance (JT Foxx, Coach). Your help, support, and encouragement are deeply appreciated. We would also like to extend a heartfelt thank you to our circle of loving family, friends, clients, and peers who have all been very supportive and encouraging to us.

- CONTENTS -

- INTRODUCTION - 1

Chapter - 1 - ....
The Unknowns 5

Chapter - 2 - ....
Skillset Diversification 11

Chapter - 3 - ....
Tame Stress 19

Chapter - 4 - ....
Assess Risk 31

Chapter - 5 - ....
Raise your Wealth 43

Chapter - 6 - ....
DOMinating Fear of Unknowns 55

- FINAL THOUGHTS - 59

- INTRODUCTION -

Fong and I had just gone to our first real estate event. We were excited to attend the three-day event to learn what we needed to start our path to financial freedom via real estate. We dreamt about how we would no longer have to worry about losing our engineering jobs should the oil and gas industry plummet; about how we can help out our families, especially the ones overseas or those that aren't as well off; and how we can finally make a bigger and better impact on our community. Things will be great!

Fast forward to the three-day course – we had learned so much, yet we realized there was still so much we needed to know to get us to where we wanted to be. We had no idea that there was so much to real estate. We needed more education to get where we wanted to go. To help our families, friends, and community and to live life on our own terms, not what our bosses tell us to do. We were scared out of our minds. We had just signed up for what we felt was a HUGE cost to learn the advanced techniques of real estate investing. It didn't matter though, our dreams and desires told us it was the right thing to do.

As we continued to learn about real estate, and a lot of other investment and business strategies over the years, we have now reached a level where we are building a great financial empire with real estate, investments and other businesses. Looking back, we were SHOCKED to see how much time and money we were spending on courses, books, and speaking. We found that to become an entrepreneur there was a lot of elements that we had worked on to become who we are today and to achieve what we want to achieve in the future. Indirectly we realized that we had massively increased and diversified our skillsets, that we were able to control and tame our stress levels, we became much better at assessing risk, and while doing so, raised our wealth to *Make More and Work Less*. We looked even further back on who we were before we worked on these elements and discovered what it really was, that held us back...FEAR. Fear of the unknown, fear of the "What If's", and fear of failure. One word comes to mind when we thought back to putting in our very first real estate offer...TERRIFIED! Even if we knew we would be getting a great deal, we were absolutely scared of having it accepted. Many years later, having more skills and financial literacy, we see now that although the fear of the unknown can never be eliminated, it can truly be challenged, faced, and dominated. Dominating fear is a trait that opens up the path way to *Make More and Work Less*.

Through this book, we will share with you strategies and tips as to how you can manage your risks, take calculated high risks and turn them into rewards. We dive deep into how diversifying your skillsets can open up opportunities exponentially. We demonstrate how our minds perceive stress and how we can use it to maximize the positive impact. Finally, we illustrate how wealth is applied to all aspects of our lives and how wealth, especially team and financial wealth can set you free. We hope that this will give you a chance to see for yourself how important it is to dominate your fears of the unknown and grow while doing so.

Although this is but an introduction to the importance of dominating your fears, by skillset diversification, taming stress, assessing risk, and raising wealth, we hope that it will open your minds to explore what your unlocked potential is. By applying the skills that you learn to your everyday life, it can lead you to succeed and *Make More and Work Less.*

We sincerely hope that you will use your new-found skills to help your community and those in it. As Napoleon Hill put it, "It is literally true that you can succeed best and quickest by helping others succeed".

Now, let's get into the keys of the book!

Thank you and enjoy!

Chapter - 1 -
The Unknowns

Do you or someone you know around you, feel insecure with their jobs? Or even dread the jobs that they are in? Or maybe you feel that you were meant to do more, offer more, and make more. If that is the case, with you or those around you, why not do something about it? Some people wake up every morning, WISHING to sleep in, WISHING to skip work, and WISHING to go on vacation. However, when asked, "Why don't you?" They usually say things like: "Well, I need to work, that's life, what else can I do?" What they are really saying is "I am afraid of the unknown."

We are afraid of jumping out of our comfort zone. We are fearful of doing something different. Fearful of being <u>seen</u> as different. That fear of the unknown is what is holding most people back from unlocking their potential. It imprisons us in our own minds, and prevents us from the freedom of becoming a star. We look around and see that everyone else is in the same situation and when we talk to each other we feel comfortable, we feel we are a part of something, because we are all dealing with the same thing. Once someone says they want to make a change, everyone around, tells them things like: "It won't work", "you can't do that", or "it's easy to say…wait till you do it", or "who do you think you are?"

Nothing New

Think back to when you did something different for the first time. Whether it is learning how to drive a car, going to your first job interview, even trying that new restaurant down the street. Whether it was something big or small there was a hint of the unknown. There was a fear of what might happen. What if the food isn't good? What if I scratch the car? What if I say the wrong thing? Even with all those fears, all those unknowns, you would find a way to overcome them and rise to the challenge. You would find out what is needed to get ready for that interview, check reviews on the restaurant, train your mind to relax, or have back up plans in place if things do not go your way. More often than not, regardless of the outcome of the challenge, you would have come out of it better than when you got into it. You could have succeeded with flying colors, or you could have learned something from the experience that would put you in a better position the next time you take on a challenge. What is interesting is that when it comes to travelling to a new destination, learning to drive, trying new foods, etc. it is something that happens to us all the time, but when it comes to our careers, our finances, and our dreams, we tend to shy away from applying those steps and just accept that sticking with the norm is the way it should be.

Breaking Out

It is true that breaking out of the norm is no easy task, but the results are never disappointing. You will look back and say: "Wow! Look how far I have come. I'm so glad I challenged that fear!" The truth is that we are all anxious with regards to our futures. There is no escape from the fear of the unknown. However, there are ways to make it easier to deal with, easier to face, and more likely to succeed when going up against the unknown. We must all: **S**killset diversify, **T**ame our stress, **A**ssess the risks, **R**aise our wealth, and then we will **DOM**inate the fear from the unknowns, hereby...creating our OWN gateway to freedom.

Throughout this book we will discuss keys, strategies, and the 'WHY" behind the importance of: Skillset diversification,

MAKE MORE WORK LESS by Creating your Gateway to STARDOM

Taming your Stress, Assessing your Risks, and Raising your Wealth. You will discover how applying some simple strategies will have you more prepared for the unknown, more confident in stepping out of your comfort zone, and ultimately dominating your fears. When these fears are challenged then you can truly *Make More and Work Less.*

Chapter - 2 -
Skillset Diversification

MAKE MORE WORK LESS by Creating your Gateway to STARDOM

Think back to when you first learned how to drive or ride a bike. Now imagine that you delivered papers or flyers. What would your options be if you didn't know how to ride a bike or drive? You are limited to your ability to walk and can only cover a certain distance within a period of time that you have available. Now if you were paid $1 for every flyer delivered, what would you make? Now imagine how many more flyers you can deliver if you acquired the skill of riding a bike. What happens when you can drive a car to an apartment complex or a stretch of townhomes? How many more flyers can you deliver then? For every skill you acquire, you open up an entire realm of opportunities. The more skills you acquire, the more diversified your skillsets are, opening yourself up to more opportunities and options. There are two types of skills you can acquire:

1) Skills that expand your current skillset
2) Skills that are completely different than your current skillset

Expanding Your Current Skillset

A person's current skillset is the most common and logical area that most people will work to expand. With our flyer delivery example, we focused on the delivery aspect of skills. Expanding from walking to biking to driving. Each enhanced skill allows for more distance, in a shorter amount of time, in return for more results. These skills are those that make you more valuable in the current job or role that you are in right now. You can go to courses, do research, and get specialized enough to enhance the skills that will allow you to make advancements in your current industry. These skills separate you from all the other people that are also in your field or industry, and what makes you more valuable than others. Going back to the delivery example, the person with the skills to drive a car would be more sought after than the person without the skill to drive.

Let's look at this from another industry. Imagine yourself as an engineer working with steel and concrete structures. Just like all the other engineers, you have the same education and the same degrees and therefore you all have the same roles and/or positions in the industry. To get ahead of your fellow engineers, you can specialize in dynamic analysis, sharpen your skills with the newest design software, and attend regular seminars on new construction advancements and technology. Having these new skills will separate you from those who do not enhance their current skillsets. It will position you for possible promotions or more senior roles. All in all, it makes you a stronger and more valuable engineer.

These skills open up options for different engineering companies if your current company is not a good fit for you. They prepare you for possible restructuring as you will be an asset that the company would like to hold onto over others. These enhancements also sets you up as the expert and/or authority in those aspects of the industry. However these skillsets, although very important to expand on, does not have much impact if the industry itself starts to suffer or if you do not enjoy the industry itself. The only opportunities that these enhancements will open will be in the industry and it will not prepare you for possible ventures outside of said industry. Which brings us to the second set of skills: brand new skills outside of your industry. It is these skills that will increase your options and opportunities exponentially!

Diversifying Outside Skillsets

Let's imagine that while delivering flyers you decide to learn about wholesaling real estate properties. Something completely different than delivering flyers, but also something that you can do while you are delivering flyers. While you are delivering flyers you can be scouting for potential buy, fix and flip properties, properties that may be in foreclosure, or build relationships in the community to get first-hand information on potential motivated sellers. As you are sharpening your skills as an expert wholesaler, there will come a time where you can decide to continue with delivering flyers or structure wholesaling properties full time. This would be an opportunity that would not have opened up if you had not diversified your skillset outside of the delivery industry. Not only does that allow you to enter an entire different industry, it also allows for opportunities within your current industry. Since you are delivering flyers anyways, why not pass out flyers with your contact information in case people are looking to sell their property. You could also potentially secure additional delivery contracts which you can now delegate or sub contract out to other delivery companies, which is similar to what you are currently doing with contracts while wholesaling properties. The added bonus to this new skillset is that if anything happens to the delivery industry you can always go fully into another industry hereby protecting you from a potential unknown.

Unfortunately most people are too afraid, lazy, or short sighted to see the value or the potential of diversifying their skills outside their industry. They look at others who are either just following along with their current roles or enhancing their industry skills, and feel that they should also just follow along and shouldn't do anything different than everyone else. They come up with excuses and other reasons as to why they don't need the different skills. The reality is, it is these different skillsets that really separate you from everyone else. When applied to your current industry, you will now be even more valuable than anyone else. It is this diversification that opens up the most opportunities and options for you. The more options you have, the less fearful you are with the unknown.

Imagine that engineer diversifying into entrepreneurship, acquiring the skillsets of business, investing, and public speaking. Throughout the process the engineer sharpens their skills in effective hand gestures, creating courses on business strategies and branding. Not only will this engineer have the option to do business coaching full time or fulfill speaking engagements but by applying those skills as an engineer, they now become an engineer with assets that no other engineer has. They are better at building relationships, conducting presentations, and training other engineers.

The more diversified in skills you are, the more creative you will find yourself. Your attention to details become enhanced and your confidence will grow. You will start to mix and match different skillsets from different industries and that will result in exponential growth and options.

How to Start

One of the most common questions when one realizes that they need to diversify their skillset is: "What skills should I acquire?" That really depends on what you want to do and what interests you have. For instance, if you want to acquire more business skills you may want to consider some business classes or workshops. Surround yourself with people that have the skillsets that you want to acquire. Listen to podcasts or read books/articles by experts in that field. The key is to be consistent and persistent in acquiring those skills.

First step to STARDOM

As you can see, simply diversifying your skillsets, has astronomical results in your ability to face the unknown.

Ask Yourself:

- What new skills can I acquire?
- What do I enjoy learning about?
- What opportunities can open up if I acquired that new skill?
- Imagine all the opportunities that can open up if I simply learn a new language / music / business / etc.?

The possibilities are endless and the results are phenomenal!

**The first step to
Creating your Gateway to STARDOM
by Dominating the Fear of Unknowns:**

SKILLSET DIVERSIFICATION

Chapter - 3 -
Tame Stress

MAKE MORE WORK LESS by Creating your Gateway to STARDOM

You now know the importance of diversifying your skillsets, not only within your industry but in other industries as well. Talk about facing the unknown! Now what's that feeling when we are faced with the unknown? – STRESS. Remember when you were sitting in class getting ready to take your year-end exam? What will the questions be? What will the weight of the questions be? What percentage of the final grade will this exam be worth? All unknowns. And how did you feel? Anxious, scared, sweaty, panic, all the above? Those are all characteristics that most people associate with stress. However stress can be good or bad. Without a form of stress, nothing really happens. No stress – no motivation, no stress – no movement, no stress – no progress. It is unfortunate that in our society today most people associate stress as a negative element to our lives. We often hear: "I'm stressed out", "I would, but I'm afraid it would really stress me out", or "YOU ARE STRESSING ME OUT!" How stress affects you is totally up to you to decide. Whether you view the stress as positive or negative all depends on what your comfort level and confidence level is. For instance, if you studied for that exam, reviewed the information daily, did all the practice exams, and did all the assignments throughout the year, you would feel pretty confident in yourself knowing the material and not really be stressed while doing the exam. In fact you would be positively stressed to see how well you did and excited to get it done. Whereas someone who is not prepare, did not study, and did not attend class would wish the exam will never come – negative stress.

What is also happening in our society more often than not, is that people are allowing themselves to feel negative stress. How do you allow yourself to feel stressed? You may ask. As we mentioned before, stress is generally seen negatively, and therefore when people say "I'm stressed" it is generally in a negative context. The instant people say "I'm stressed" they are justifying in their minds that they are stressed negatively. They are fueling that negative sense of stress simply by saying it out loud and telling other people. The more they say it, the more they feel it, and the more they allow negative stress to build. What we must do when faced with the element of stress, is tame it beforehand so that only positive stress occurs.

What is Stress?

Contrary to what people think. Stress is not a feeling. It is an occurrence.

Stress is the change from any balance state.

When someone is pulling your arm, the stress is the elongation of your arm from a balanced resting state to a stretched out state. What you feel is the stretch, the pull, the 'stressed' cells to reach the desired results. How much stress you feel is related to your tolerance of change from your comfort state. What most people do not realize is that comfort state expands which allows for higher stress tolerance.

Our bodies go through stress all the time. From our perspective it is not stressful because we are comfortable with it, we know what to expect. While we take a shower, our bodies go through massive stress. Just think of the time you got out of the hot tub and jumped back into the pool...IT'S COLD!!! But even so we adapt to that new temperature and it becomes our new "comfort zone". This is no different than what our minds go through. When we experience something new or different, we go through stress due to the unknown. However once you experience it, you cannot un-experience it, and it becomes your new "comfort zone". One way to tame stress is to experience what is currently an unknown to you, which means facing change.

Pain or Pleasure

Change is measured by different levels of pain or pleasure. The position on where the pain and pleasure spectrum the change is perceived to be, will determine how willing an individual is to face the change. Imagine that you have a dental appointment tomorrow morning at 7AM. The fact that you had to change your wakeup time from 7AM to 5:30AM in the morning to prepare to go to the dentist would be a "painful" change. Not only do you not want to go, you will also likely encounter some pain during the visit. These are all changes that you are unlikely to want. However, if you are actually boarding a flight to Hawaii at 7AM, then even a wakeup time of 3:30AM is not a problem. In fact, you cannot wait to wake up at 3:30AM in the morning! Which brings us to the wise words of Nido Qubein:

> *"People will only change when the pain of remaining the same is greater than the pain of change."*

Based on that, if you were in great pain due to a toothache, you couldn't be more happy going to the dentist regardless of time of day. Similarly you would be pretty stressed out if you are to wake up early the next morning to get to an exam that you are not prepared for. This demonstrates that negative and positive stress is determined by us. We decided what energy to give it, what meaning it has, and what story it develops. This is all due to the difference in change. If we were to be comfortable with change then change becomes the norm. The negative stress goes away. The more comfortable we are with change, the more the stress becomes positive, a motivation or even a challenge. When we view change as good and positive stress, we start to want it more often and NOT have our futures be just the repetition of our past. Let's look closer to see what good and bad stress does to us.

Bad Stress

This is normally known as negative stress or in general – stress. These are the stresses that stops you in your tracks. Think back to the first time you jumped into a pool, you may have walked up to it a few times before you bundled up the courage to dive in. The first few times that you attempted to dive in but did not is due to the negative stress. This stress cannot be 100% taken care of, it can however be minimized, reduced and handled by experience, time, and knowledge. The stress will always exist because as humans, when our safety is challenged, we will enter the fight, flight or freeze modes. Challenge or Run or Stay Still. When bad stress overpowers the good stress, it triggers our fears and we run or freeze. Usually it is our mental and/or emotional safety that is in question. Very rarely are we actually in physical danger. When we feel that we do not have control, are not prepared, or facing something different and are afraid of the unknown, that is when negative stress takes course. One of the most common habits that we have that allows that negative stress to loom is letting things run its course. Not working on a project as the days go by when suddenly it is due the next day. Not exercising one day after another until one day you realized you gained a few pounds. Not looking at your finances on a consistent basis until one day you realized you did not do enough for retirement. These delays and many others are ways in which negative stress builds momentum and strength. To combat this habit, we must take control of our daily routines and habits, diversify our skillsets on a regular basis, and welcome change as a challenge or an opportunity to grow. By doing so strategically, we will soon feel that the bad stresses reduce and control is gained. That is when good stress takes over.

Good Stress

Good and positive stress is like tension in a bow. Without stressing the bow, the arrow will not hit its target. Without stress we will not be challenged, there would be no achievements, no motivation, no progress, and no success. We would ultimately be bored with our lives. What was the best movie that you have watched recently? Why was it so good? Why was it so memorable? It was likely because it stressed you in a positive way. Remember when you played a game of cards or a board game? The excitement and the challenge of winning made it fun and invigorating. These are all positive stresses. These stresses motivate and inspire you to do it again or tackle something else that is a little challenging.

Positive Experience/Stress → Exciting Vision → Motivating Image of Yourself Succeeding!

For example, running a marathon is not exactly an easy task. You run the 5km race and you felt good about it. Then you see yourself completing the 10km in your head. You see yourself challenging the ½ marathon. After succeeding and experiencing the thrill of crossing the finish line of the ½ marathon, you start to see the possibility of the full marathon in your grasp. The motivating stress challenges you, inspires you, and soon enough you cross the finish line of the full marathon. Positive stress gets you out of ruts. You start seeing the positives, the opportunities, and the growth in outcomes and changes. The stress and pain become a pleasure and challenge as you focus on the results.

Stress → Motivation → Action → Success → Confidence

Stress can be a powerful weapon as long as you give it the right energy. Whether you feed it with negative or positive energy is up to you. So why not use it to strengthen yourself?

10 Keys to Taming Stress

1) Be Comfortable with Change: change your scenery, find new hobbies/interests, and acquire new skills.

2) Relax and Take Breaks: Reward yourself for a job well done.

3) Be Organized:
Purposeful Action → Developed Plan → Control

4) You are Not Alone: There is probably someone who has done what you want to do. Share stories, ask questions, and gain perspective. Have a team around you.

5) Honesty Conquers Stress: The more excuses you make the more stress builds, be honest with yourself. Ex. "I may not be perfect, but parts of me are excellent." Tell people what bothers you so that you can set the stage as to what is expected of yourself and of others. Accept the situation and ask "what's next?" By doing so you will set the ball up into the future's court, instead of being fixated on the current circumstances. Allowing yourself to challenge the future, opens the mind up for creativity as you explore the possibilities of the future before it comes, instead of facing it unprepared.

6) Stress Arises from Perceived Challenges: Too many times we allow our subconscious minds to dictate what to believe. Trust but verify what you believe, because things may not always be what they seem. The more you approach challenges by asking questions and finding out more, the less negative stress you will have with the challenge.

7) Choose your Battles: Not all battles/challenges need to be won or faced. Have your end goals in sight, you may need to lose some battles or pass on some challenges to win the war.

8) Shut out Unnecessary Noise: Focus on the task at hand. Prioritize decisions/tasks that need to be done. Clear your head while making a decision.

9) Stress Reduction Strategies: Have a routine that is set for creating habits. For instance, creating the habit of working out every morning or doing some

reading every night will prevent the stress of asking yourself the question "should I run today? Or do some reading tonight?" Creating these routines along with gestures or sayings when stressed will allow you to calm your mind. For example, close your eyes, take a deep breath and count to 5 when feeling stressed, or clap your hands to pump yourself up when feeling overwhelmed. Whatever it is that will get you out of your current negative stressed state into a motivating positive state.

10) <u>Learn to Laugh</u>: Always find the fun in all you do. We all grow and learn better when we are enjoying ourselves, having fun, and laughing. You most likely learned more about business and real estate investing playing the game monopoly than reading a textbook. Being able to laugh at ourselves is a great way to view situations from another perspective. Just think of the stories that great comedians tell, many of these stories may have been the worst day of their lives, but by finding the humor in the story, they are able to enjoy the story and share the experience with others.

Second step to STARDOM

By taming your stress, you will be able to view stress from a positive mindset. Applying the 10 keys will get you more comfortable with change, which in turn will become positive and motivating stress. That motivating stress, like the bow string will shoot you to success, and lead to confidence.

Comfortable with Change → Motivating Stress → Action → Success → Confidence

MAKE MORE WORK LESS by Creating your Gateway to STARDOM

With the new confidence you will surely *Make More and Work Less.*

**The Second step to
Creating your Gateway to STARDOM
by Dominating the Fear of Unknowns:**

Taming Stress

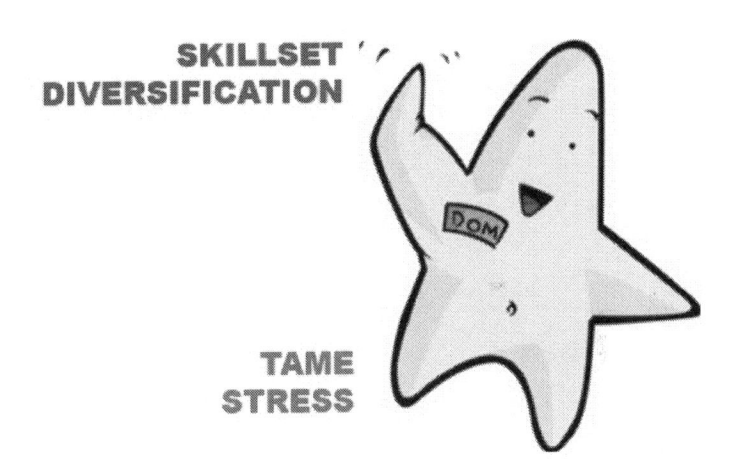

**SKILLSET
DIVERSIFICATION**

**TAME
STRESS**

Chapter - 4 -
Assess Risk

MAKE MORE WORK LESS by Creating your Gateway to STARDOM

Now that we understand the opportunities of skillset diversification and the power of taming our stress, we now need to assess the risk effectively before we make a decision. Stress and risk goes hand in hand. The higher the risk, the higher the stress, and as we have discovered, the higher the reward. Similar to stress, risk cannot be eliminated or avoided, it can only be managed. As we diversify our skillsets and control our stress we will be better equipped to assess risk. The more risk we take, the more successes we gain, leading to more confidence and skills. It all goes full circle. Negative stress stops us in our tracks, the fear of failure/taking risks can be crippling. By contrast the commitment to success and taking calculated risks is energizing and courageous. When we are energized and courageous anything can happen. So how do we take calculated risks?

What We Must Do When We Face Risk

There are a series of questions that we must ask when facing any potential risk:

1. What is the best thing that can happen as a result of taking this action?

2. What is the worst thing that can happen as a result of taking this action?

3. What is the most likely thing to happen as a result of taking this action?

4. Will taking this action take me closer to my vision?

5. Can I handle the worst case?

6. Am I willing to accept the worst case for a shot at the best case?

By asking and answering these questions we are able to place ourselves into the future and assess whether we are able to take on the risk or not. It is now a calculated risk, in which you have weighed all the outcomes, benefits, potential pitfalls, and even back up strategies if things do not go according to plan. It is a very high level assessment on the risk and a great start to your plan if you choose to go through with the risk.

First Step to Managing Risk – Plan

As we mentioned in the above section, simply asking yourself those 6 questions will give you a great start to your plan. Contrary to what most people think, coming up with a great plan starts from the end, not the beginning. The first thing we do when planning is envisioning that we have already completed it, getting the results that we want, and then work backwards. Imagine planning a wedding, what is the first thing you would do? Is it send out invitations? Book the venue? Secure hotels and flights for family and friends? No, you decide on the date. Once you know the target date you can work backwards and map out how to make everything happen the way you envisioned it.

That vision allows you to specify your actions. What is interesting is that as you specify your action you are bringing your vision closer to reality. As more of your vision becomes a reality, momentum builds, confidence increases, and risk is reduced. How often have you heard people tell you that they will get something done sooner or later? Now how often is it "sooner" rather than "later?" or worse, "forgotten?" Having a timetable will allow you to strategically map out your path to success. Reducing the risks as you envision each step. On top of that, a timetable to hold you and others accountable and is measurable so that you know whether you are on track or not. As you map out your timetable you will encounter many risks, in which you will ask the series of questions throughout. This will allow you to anticipate as many "What If" scenarios that you and your team can come up with. No matter how well you plan or envision all scenarios you can never plan for ALL scenarios. Something unexpected will always happen, which is why it is so important to be comfortable with change and have your stress tamed.

For example, you would not plan a wedding by saying we'll have a wedding sooner or later. You would break the event down, with multiple goals, milestones, priorities, and strategies. You would have plans within plans, back up scenarios, and timelines so that if the unexpected happened you will have the best possible opportunity to deal with the unexpected.

Plans

Planning is a key component to success. Imagine what it would be like if someone told you to visit a place you've never seen and you had no access to a map. You would feel lost wouldn't you? It's the same thing as planning to be successful without having a way to get there.

Let's say you want to have one cashflowing property in two months. What must you do to get there? How many offers do you have to make? How many places do you have to see? How many calls do you have to make? Just work backwards from your goals and you will have a plan. Remember, as George S. Patton once said:

> *"A good plan violently executed now is better than a perfect plan executed next week."*

So start with a plan and adjust it as you move along.

Set yearly, monthly, and daily goals and activities. Review your goals every day and plan what you want to accomplish the next day. This will allow you to wake up ready to go! You will have a plan as to what you need to do and when you need to finish it.

Remember back in school when the teacher tells you that you'll have a test on the 15th? When do you study? The 13th? The 14th? The morning of the 15th? What happens when the teacher tells you that the test is postponed until the 20th? When would you study then? If you were to plan ahead and set aside some time every day to review and study the material, would you ever be anxious as to when the test will be? Would you ever need to pull an all nighter to study for the test last minute? Having a plan in place will allow you to focus and manage your energy and time. You will no longer be wasting time thinking of what you need to do or if you have forgotten anything.

Goals

Setting goals allow you to strive for something. While goals are great, many goals are unattained mainly because people are not capable of setting goals correctly. People set goals that are too unachievable in the time period they want. Their goals would be too vague. They would also have no timeline. Let's look at these a little more closely and find out how we can avoid these mistakes.

If the goal is too grand, the possibility of failure is great. For example, if your goal for this year is to have 10 cashflow properties when you don't have any properties or knowledge at all, then the chances of success are very slim. Have goals that are challenging yet achievable.

If a goal is too vague, then one will never know if the goal is reached or not. For example, if one were to say: "I want an investment", what does that mean? What kind? How many? Does buying one silver coin count? Are you going into stocks? Real estate? However, if one were to say "I want a cashflowing single family property to bring in a positive cashflow of at least $500 monthly by April next year," then, we know exactly what is wanted and when that goal is achieved.

Finally if a goal has no timeline, then it will never get done. Think back to the tests that your teachers gave you. If they never told you a date, would you ever have studied for an undisclosed date? Probably not. Without a date, goals tend to be pushed aside and forgotten. The power of having dates will also allow you to work backwards and set mini goals and dates for you to meet your goals. For example, if your goal is to have 10 cashflowing properties by the end of the year, then you may have a goal of attaining five in six months. When six months comes around and you have five properties, then you know that you are on track to meet your annual goal. This way you can break down your plan into one year goals, 6 month goals, monthly goals, weekly and, daily goals.

After setting your goals, you will find that planning and strategizing your actions become easier and easier. This may be an overwhelming task to begin with and therefore we highly recommend you seek the help of a coach or a mentor.

Goals turn risks into rewards. You should have long term, medium, short, and immediate goals in all aspects of your life: Physical, emotional, spiritual, mental, social, civic, family, career, education, financial, and the list goes on. The shorter the timeline the more specific the goal should be. In addition to timeline goals, each goal should have three levels of desired outcomes: **Acceptable**, **Preferred**, and **Outstanding**.

> Acceptable – What is the minimum results that you will be content about?

> Preferred – What is the target that you would like to achieve?

> Outstanding – What would be a result that will leave you breathless?

For example: Let's imagine that you would like to learn a new language. You may feel that a goal to be fluent in Spanish in 6 months, is too grand a goal to set for yourself. However you can set the following:

> Acceptable – In three months I would like to have completed 3 levels of Spanish classes.

Preferred – In six months I would like to be able to have a conversation with a Spanish speaking individual.

Outstanding – In nine months I would like to be able to get around in Spain speaking only Spanish even though it is not fluent.

By creating 3 goal levels, you will be motivated as you achieve each level, most likely earlier than you thought. In addition, you will feel good and excited about achieving each level, giving you more momentum to reach the next level or create new ones.

4 Benefits of Goal Setting

Time → Energy → Talent → Skill

As mentioned earlier, goals and planning allow for a timetable to be constructed, paving way to having a system to track progress and successes. As each milestone is reached successfully or small successes within the project is reached, morale and excitement increases, and momentum is created, leading to higher energy levels. As your energy level increases, you will realize where you and your team's talents are, while you celebrate the achievements. With the talents strengthened, efficiencies will be challenged and new skills will be acquired automatically to reach these efficiencies. All of that will then result in meeting timetables earlier and the cycle feeds itself. Soon you will have bigger goals identified and results measured. These results will allow for adjustments in advance for future projects or allow obstacles to be identified earlier in the process.

Third step to STARDOM

By strategically setting goals and creating plans, it is obvious what impact they have in assessing risk. The more effective you are at goals and plans, the more capable you are with assessing risk and in turn taming stress and ultimately dominating the fear of the unknown.

Ask Yourself:

- What is the: Best, Worse, and Most Likely case if I take this action?
- Am I closer to my Vision?
- Am I willing to accept the worse case for a shot at the best case?

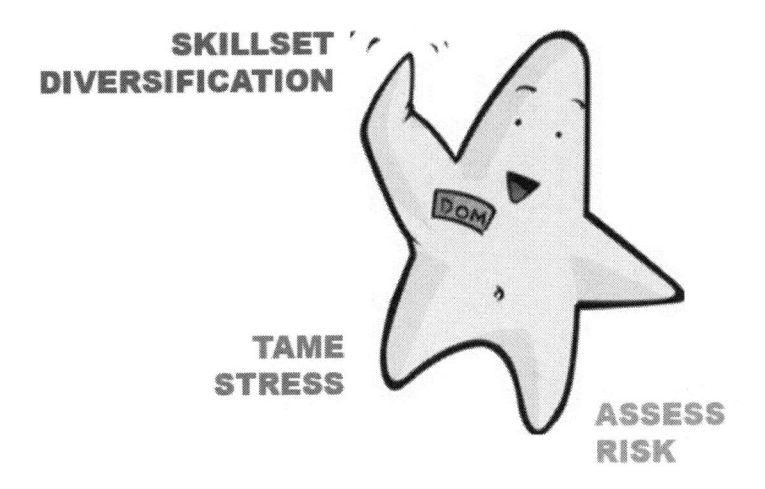

MAKE MORE WORK LESS by Creating your Gateway to STARDOM

The Third step to Creating your Gateway to STARDOM by Dominating the Fear of Unknowns:

Assess Risk

SKILLSET
DIVERSIFICATION

TAME
STRESS

ASSESS
RISK

Chapter - 5 -
Raise Wealth

When it comes to the word WEALTH, most people think about financial wealth. However, wealth can be applied to all areas in our lives. Physical wealth, educational wealth, relationship wealth, family wealth, spiritual wealth, knowledge, skills, team, and the list goes on. All areas of wealth should be powered by one element, your WHY.

Why are you working on this goal? Why is this so important to you? Why keep working on it when it's so hard? Why, why, why? Your why is what will keep driving you on when things are getting you down and your attitude and confidence in yourself are no longer enough. If your why doesn't make you cry, keep working on finding it.

Your why becomes your mission and is the foundation of what you are building. If your foundation is weak, then what you are building will crumble in a matter of time. If your foundation is strong, no matter what wind or hardship is blowing on you, you hold the key to rebuilding because your foundation is still there.

To help you with your "Why" think about the following statement:

> *"If time and money is of no concern to me, and I know I cannot fail: what would I be, do, help with, and leave behind?"*

The more wealth in all aspects of your life that you have, the more freedom you will have. If you have spectacular health, risks of diseases and health scares would not be too high on your mind as you already have great health. You already have the routines and habits that allow you to combat potential problems, and you would be very knowledgeable in the health area to make the right decisions to deal with any health issues. Wealth in health leaves you with more freedom to concentrate on building other areas of wealth like financial and/or relationships. Let's say you wanted to increase your relationship wealth, then you will start building it by diversifying your skillsets in that area. Going to more networking events, working on your public speaking skills, focusing on adding value to others, etc. until one day you realize that you have relationship wealth. As you can see, building wealth requires all the previous three steps: Skillset Diversification, Taming Stress, and Assessing Risks. Slowly but surely your wealth in all aspects will grow. As your wealth grows, you will have less to fear, less unknowns and in turn more freedom.

What is Freedom Worth?

After defining what wealth can be applied to, many of us understand the importance of health, education, and relationship wealth. What is interesting is that most people do not spend a lot of time learning about the traditional sense of wealth – Financial Wealth. Ironically the one wealth that has the most impact on all the other wealth and also your overall freedom, is Financial Wealth. More of us need to understand and increase our financial literacy. Too often, we just follow what most people are doing, what our parents are doing, and what our friends are doing. Unfortunately in most cases it is the blind leading the blind. What has worked for our parents, may not work for us now. Our friends may not fully understand themselves what they are doing. The general public tends to spend more time reading about entertainment and sports than what new strategies there are to warehouse your financial wealth.

Now just like everything else, there is a price to acquire this wealth, the price of time, effort, and funds. We must all calculate the risks of all opportunities, investments, and financial education. To be able to assess those risks we must ask ourselves:

"What does Financial Wealth and Freedom mean to me?"

After asking this question to many individuals, the following sums up all the answers:

Freedom

> **To be able to do what you want, with who you want, where ever you want, and whenever you want.**

Wouldn't you say that covers it all? Now where did we see something similar to that? When we talked about what our 'Why' is. See how financial freedom goes hand in hand with what your 'Why' is? As a society we must start to understand what an expense is, and what an investment in ourselves is. Is what you are about to do getting you closer to your vision, your goal, and your 'Why'? If that applies to your financial freedom, ask yourself:

How long can I go without working?
How much do I need for retirement?
How long would it take for me to get there?
Will this action get me closer to retirement in a shorter amount of time?
Will this allow me the freedom I dream of?

Unfortunate Reality

There are so many cases now where individuals need to go back to work after retirement because they did not have enough saved up. Many households don't even have any savings. The main reason why is that they do not spend the time to ask the right questions, to diversify their skills, to challenge the unknown and face the fear. It is becoming more and more evident that for one to retire at the age of 65, one requires multiple streams of income.

Whether it is with real estate, business, commodities, network marketing, exempt markets, stocks, and/or infinite banking, there are many options one can choose from to create the options for early freedom. Whatever it is, it will require you to decide what your 'Why' is and how you are going to achieve it. Then you can obtain the skills, the motivating stress, the assessing of risk, and finally the wealth. With that newfound wealth you will have more freedom and create even more wealth in all aspects of your life.

For more information on investment strategies read our books:

Make More Work Less – The Guide to Unlocking your Potential to Live and Work on Your Own Terms

Make More Work Less with CASHFLOW – The Step by Step Keys to Finding, Acquiring, and Maintaining Cashflow Investment Properties

Team Wealth

With all the opportunities out there, all the skills that can be acquired, it is virtually impossible for one to do it all themselves. Which brings us to another very important wealth, Team Wealth. There isn't enough time in the day for us to be learning everything to the point where we are competent enough to make the right decisions or stay current enough to make the most informed decision. Why not seek the advice or the expertise of a professional that deals with these situations every day? Experts who need to educate themselves to be relevant in the industry. Professionals who can do the job faster and more creatively than we can. Advisers who have the experience to know what to do if a unique situation arises. To *Make More* and *Work Less*, we cannot rely on one person. We must build a team that we can trust. When we have the team of experts, not only are we able to ensure that our questions or problems are looked after, it also allows us the time to concentrate on what we do best.

We are always reminded of the story of Henry Ford, the founder of Ford, when we talk about teams. The following is an excerpt from the book *Think and Grow Rich* by Napoleon Hill [1938].

> *During the world war, a Chicago newspaper published certain editorials in which, among other statements, Henry Ford was called "an ignorant pacifist." Mr. Ford objected to the statements and brought suit against the paper for libeling him. When the suit was tried in the courts, the attorneys for the paper pleaded justification, and placed Mr. Ford, himself, on the witness stand, for the purpose of*

proving to the jury that he was ignorant. The attorneys asked Mr. Ford a great variety of questions, all of them intended to prove, by his own evidence, that, while he might possess considerable specialized knowledge pertaining to the manufacture of automobiles, he was, in the main, ignorant.

Mr. Ford was plied with such questions as the following:

"Who was Benedict Arnold?" and "How many soldiers did the British send over to America to put down the Rebellion of 1776?" In answer to the last question, Mr. Ford replied, "I do not know the exact number of soldiers the British sent over, but I have heard that it was a considerably larger number than ever went back."

Finally, Mr. Ford became tired of this line of questioning, and in reply to a particularly offensive question, he leaned over, pointed his finger at the lawyer who had asked, and said, "If I should really WANT to answer the foolish question you have just asked, or any of the other questions you have been asking me, let me remind you that I have a row of electric push-buttons on my desk, and by pushing the right button, I can summon to my aid men who can answer ANY question I desire to ask concerning the business to which I am devoting most of my efforts. Now, will you kindly tell me, WHY I should clutter up my mind with general knowledge, for the purpose of being able to answer questions, when I have men around me who can supply any knowledge I require?"

Even the great Henry Ford doesn't know everything himself! What is important, is knowing where to seek the knowledge when it is needed. If you want to *Make More* and *Work Less*, then you need to build a team so that you get the support and expertise when needed.

What makes a team? Relationships. Companies and sport teams have team building events and socials. If you want to have the support and the dynamics of a team you must invest into the individuals that make up that team. You cannot expect your Realtor to think of you when a great deal comes up, if you only call them once a year asking if they have a great deal. Likewise, your coach will not attend to your questions with urgency, if you don't invest the time to find out what you can do to add value to them. What makes you more important than all your team members' other clients? Why do they need to care about you and your needs? It all comes down to building the relationship and the bond with your team members so that you get a team of professionals that have common goals and will add value to each other so that everyone's best interest is on everyone's mind. It is then that you truly have a team around you.

Your team is your relational capital, your support group, and your mastermind companions. Together you can all diversify your skillsets, tame each other's stress, assess the risks, share ideas, discuss strategies, gain perspective, learn and grow from each other. Coaches, partners, professionals, experts, family, and friends can all contribute to great team wealth. With great team wealth you will see unbelievable achievements and visions that was once a dream, become a reality.

For more information on team building read our book:

Make More Work Less by Building a TEAM – The Secrets to Selecting, Building and Maintaining an Ultimate Power Team

Fourth step to STARDOM

Wealth in all aspects of your life, be it physical, mental, knowledge, spiritual, family, social, and team will all lead you to certain degrees of freedom. The more wealth you have, the less unknowns there are. The more capable you are at managing risk, the less fear you have, and the sooner you will be able to Make More and Work Less.

The fourth step to Creating your Gateway to STARDOM by Dominating the Fear of Unknowns:

Raising Wealth

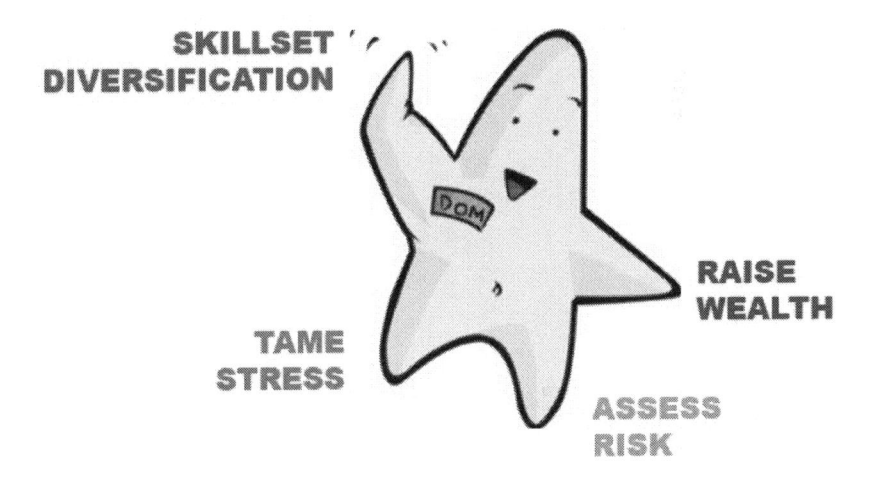

SKILLSET DIVERSIFICATION

TAME STRESS

RAISE WEALTH

ASSESS RISK

Chapter - 6 -
DOMinating Fear of Unknowns

By now you should understand:

1) How the unknown creates fear
2) The power of **Skillset Diversification**
3) The advantages of **Taming Stress**
4) The impact of **Assessing Risk** and
5) The freedom from **Raising Wealth**

These gateways, work together to **DOM**inate the fear of the unknowns. When you have the skillsets of multiple industries you are protected when certain markets are at its downturn. You open multiple doors when you can mix and match your skills, setting yourself up as someone different and irreplaceable. When you are able to tame your stress into a motivating spring board, then you will be able to challenge fears and be comfortable with change. Having the skills to assess risk, plan, and set goals effectively and strategically, will allow you avoid potential pit falls, predict outcomes, and transform risk into reward. And finally when you can obtain wealth in all shapes and forms, you open up to freedom in ways that you did not think was possible. When you have freedom, what would you be afraid of? You will have the elements to challenge, tame, assess, and collaborate with others on any unknowns. Wouldn't you say that you will now have dominated the fear of unknowns and in doing so, improve, grow, and unlock your potential? We believe that...

Today is the Day to Unlock your Potential!

Creating your Gateway to STARDOM by Dominating the Fear of Unknowns

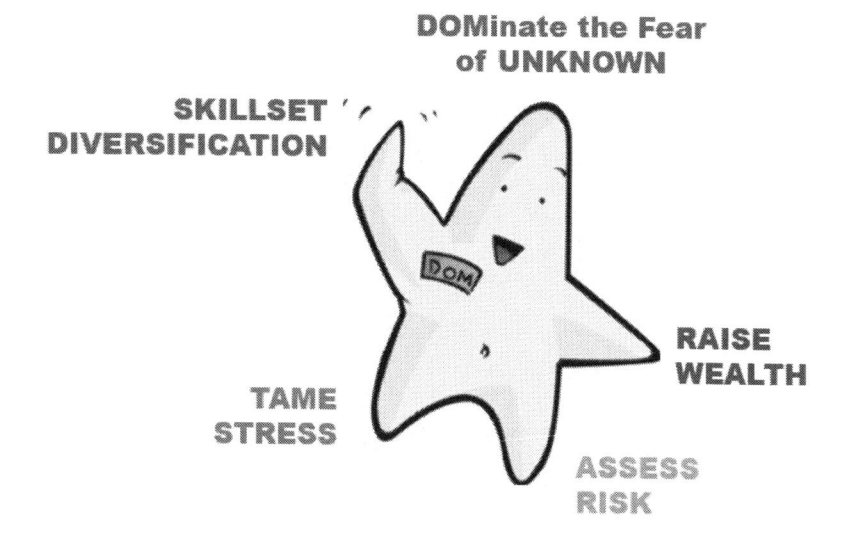

DOMinate the Fear of UNKNOWN

SKILLSET DIVERSIFICATION

TAME STRESS

RAISE WEALTH

ASSESS RISK

- FINAL THOUGHTS -

Thank you for taking the time to read our book. We have put a lot of effort into this to make it as straightforward and easily understood as a guideline on how to Make More and Work Less by Creating your Gateway to STARDOM. We felt that by adding practical tips, we could give you the keys to the problems you could encounter.

You have learned about:

1) **S**killset Diversification
2) **T**aming Stress
3) **A**ssessing Risk
4) **R**aising Wealth
5) **DOM**inating Fear of Unknowns

You might be thinking, "I read your book, what's next?" Well, that's a valid question. We've found all too often that a book, while comprehensive, sometimes leaves us with some questions we want answered. To help you move even further along, we have compiled a collection of videos from the best authorities in the market to help you. The members of our power team and our coaches have answered the most commonly asked questions in their field to add value to our treasured readers. All of which can be found on yourAREATV.

For more information on this, please visit www.yourarea.ca. If you have any questions you wish to have answered regarding this book, please feel free to e-mail us at makemoreworklessquestion@yourarea.ca. Please note that we get plenty of questions and e-mails daily, but we will do our best to answer your questions.

We will now leave you with one last quote from Dr. Phil. "Anyone can do something when they WANT to do it. Really successful people do things when they don't want to do it." So go out there and reach your dreams!

Made in the USA
Lexington, KY
23 April 2018